Congressional
Research Service
Informing the legislative debate since 1914

Armed Conflict in Syria:
Overview and U.S. Response

Christopher M. Blanchard, Coordinator
Specialist in Middle Eastern Affairs

Carla E. Humud
Analyst in Middle Eastern and African Affairs

Mary Beth D. Nikitin
Specialist in Nonproliferation

June 27, 2014

Congressional Research Service

7-5700

www.crs.gov

RL33487

Summary

Fighting continues across Syria, pitting government forces and their foreign allies against a range of anti-government insurgents, some of whom also are fighting amongst themselves. Since March 2011, the conflict has driven more than 2.8 million Syrians into neighboring countries as refugees (out of a total population of more than 22 million). Millions more Syrians are internally displaced and in need of humanitarian assistance, of which the United States remains the largest bilateral provider, with more than $2 billion in funding identified to date. The United States also has allocated a total of $287 million to date to provide nonlethal assistance to select groups.

Neither pro-Asad forces nor their opponents appear capable of achieving outright victory in the short term. Improved coordination among some anti-government forces and attrition in government ranks make a swift reassertion of state control over all of Syria unlikely. Conflict between the Islamic State of Iraq and the Levant (ISIL, a.k.a. ISIS) and other anti-Asad forces has intensified. The war in Syria is exacerbating local sectarian and political conflicts within Lebanon and Iraq, threatening national stability.

In spite of an apparent shared antipathy toward ISIL's brutality among opposition groups, many anti-Asad armed forces and their activist counterparts remain divided over tactics, strategy, and their long-term political goals for Syria. At present, the most powerful and numerous anti-Asad armed forces seek outcomes that are contrary in significant ways to stated U.S. preferences for Syria's political future. Islamist militias seeking to impose varying degrees of Sunni Islamic law on Syrian society, including members of the Islamic Front, ISIL, and Jabhat al Nusra, have marginalized others who had received U.S. assistance.

The United States and other members of the United Nations Security Council seek continued Syrian government cooperation with efforts to verifiably end Syria's chemical weapons program and provide relief. As of June 23, 2014, all of Syria's declared chemical weapons had been removed from the country. The Security Council also has endorsed principles for a negotiated settlement of the conflict that could leave members of the current Syrian government in power as members of a transitional governing body, an outcome that some opposition groups reject. Congress is considering FY2015 appropriations legislation (S. 2499) that would authorize the Administration to provide nonlethal assistance in Syria for certain purposes notwithstanding other provisions of law and prohibit the use of defense funds to provide man-portable air defense weapons (MANPADs) to entities in Syria (H.R. 4870). The Administration is seeking $2.75 billion in funding for the Syria crisis in FY2015, including $1.1 billion for humanitarian programs, $1 billion for regional stabilization, and $500 million for DOD-led arming and training of vetted opposition forces for select purposes. The Senate Armed Services Committee-reported FY2015 defense authorization bill (Section 1209 of S. 2410) would authorize such support.

The humanitarian and regional security crises emanating from Syria now appear to be beyond the power of any single actor, including the United States, to contain or fully address. Large numbers of Syrian refugees, the growth of powerful armed extremist groups in Syria, and the assertive involvement of Iran, Turkey, and Sunni Arab governments in Syria's civil war are all negatively affecting the regional security environment in the Middle East. In light of these conditions and trends, Congress is likely to face choices about the investment of U.S. relief and security assistance funding in relation to the crisis in Syria and its effects on the region for years to come. For more analysis and information, see CRS Report R42848, *Syria's Chemical Weapons: Issues for Congress*, coordinated by Mary Beth D. Nikitin, and CRS Report R43119, *Syria: Overview of the Humanitarian Response*, by Rhoda Margesson and Susan G. Chesser.

Contents

Figures

Tables

Contacts

Overview

Fighting continues across Syria, pitting government forces and their foreign allies against a range of anti-government insurgents, some of whom also are fighting amongst themselves. Government forces are fighting on multiple fronts and have lost or ceded control of large areas of the country since 2011, but hold most major cities and have advanced in key areas in recent months. The Asad government continues to receive support from Russia and Iran, and, contrary to some observers' predictions, has shown no indication of an imminent collapse. Opposition forces are formidable but lack unity of purpose, unity of command, and unified international support. Various opposition groups have, depending on the circumstances, cooperated and competed. At present, significant elements of the opposition are engaged in outright conflict against one another. Much of the armed opposition seeks to replace the Asad government with a state ruled according to some form of Sunni Islamic law, which non-Sunni minority groups oppose. Kurdish groups control areas of northeastern Syria and may seek autonomy or independence in the future.

Meanwhile, chemical weapons inspectors work to oversee and implement the terms of the September 2013 chemical disarmament agreement endorsed by the United Nations (U.N.) Security Council in Resolution 2118. Some rebel groups and regional governments have criticized the U.S. decision to forego a threatened military strike against Syrian government forces in response to the Syrian military's alleged use of chemical weapons in August. Members of Congress expressed a broad range of views regarding the potential use of force in Syria during intense debate in September, and Obama Administration officials have stated that they believe that the threat of the use of force by the United States was instrumental in convincing Syrian President Bashar al Asad to commit to the disarmament plan. Recent allegations of the use of chlorine gas by government forces have revived debates about appropriate responses.

With internationally supervised disarmament proceeding, U.S. diplomatic efforts remain committed to shaping the terms and conditions for negotiation to end the fighting and establish a transitional governing body as called for by a communiqué agreed to in Geneva in June 2012. That communiqué was further endorsed in Resolutions 2118 and 2139, and served as the basis for the January-February 2014 "Geneva II" talks in Switzerland involving some members of the Syrian opposition, representatives of the Syrian government, and delegates from dozens of countries. Those talks failed to address the establishment of a transitional body, based largely on Syrian government insistence that terrorism concerns be resolved first.

Several unarmed and armed groups rejected the Geneva II talks outright, and opposition forces remain divided over questions of whether and under what conditions to participate in negotiations with the Asad government. Advances by pro-Asad forces and opposition forces in the subsequent months have led some supporters of each side to argue for continued fighting rather than negotiation. However, neither pro-Asad forces nor their opponents appear capable of achieving outright victory in the short term. Combat between Islamic State of Iraq and the Levant (ISIL, aka ISIS)[1] and other anti-Asad forces across northern and eastern Syria has intensified since late December 2013, and in June 2014, ISIL launched a major offensive in north-central Iraq. ISIL's operations have reinvigorated U.S. debate about policy responses to conflict in both countries.

---

[1] The Islamic State of Iraq and the Levant (ISIL) also is commonly referred to in English language reports as the Islamic State of Iraq and Al Sham (ISIS). *Al Sham* is an Arabic term for the Levant. Some Syrians and others in the region refer to ISIL as "Daesh," the acronym for its name in Arabic *Ad Dawla al Islamiyya fil Iraq wa-ash Sham*.

Figure 1. Conflict Map and Regional Humanitarian Situation

(As of June 2014)

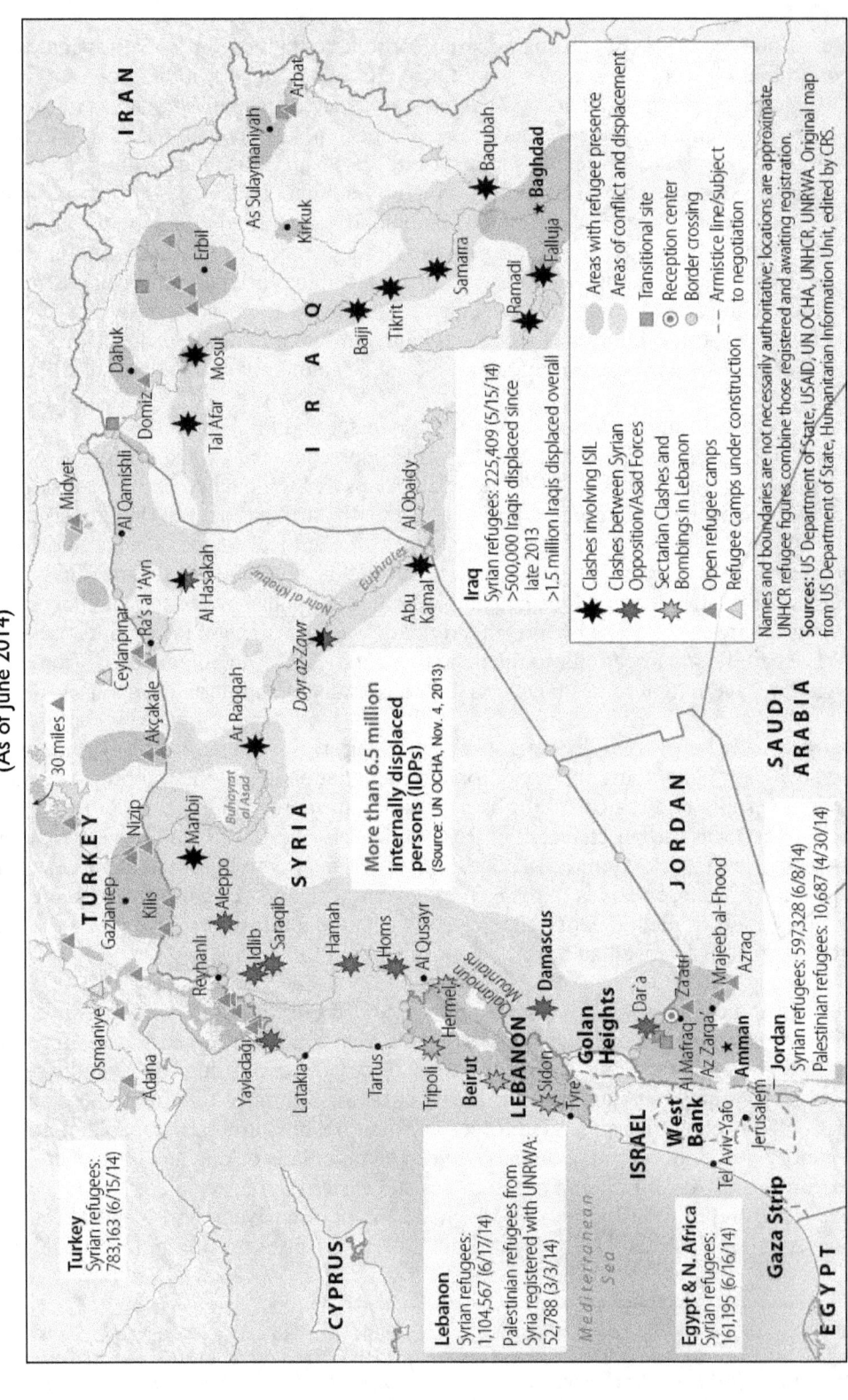

Note: Clash symbols in Syria and Iraq denote areas where recent clashes have occurred, not areas of current control.

In spite of an apparent shared antipathy among opposition groups toward ISIL's brutality, many anti-Asad armed forces and their activist counterparts remain divided over tactics, strategy, and their long-term political goals for Syria. U.S. intelligence estimates the strength of the insurgency in Syria at "somewhere between 75,000 or 80,000 or up to 110,000 to 115,000 insurgents, who are organized into more than 1,500 groups of widely varying political leanings."

As of May 2014, the most powerful and numerous anti-Asad armed forces seek outcomes that are contrary in significant ways to stated U.S. preferences for Syria's political future. Islamist militias seeking to enforce varying degrees of what they recognize as Sunni Islamic law in Syrian society—among them members of the Islamic Front (see below), ISIL, and Jabhat al Nusra— have marginalized other armed groups, including some that received U.S. assistance. U.S. intelligence community leaders have identified the approximately 26,000 members of ISIL, Jabhat al Nusra, and Ahrar al Sham (a key component of the Islamic Front) both as extremists and as the most effective opposition forces in the field. U.S. officials believe that as many as "7,500 foreign fighters from some 50 countries" have travelled to Syria, including Al Qaeda-linked veterans of previous conflicts and Western nationals.[2]

In its 2014 threat assessment testimony, the U.S. intelligence community judged that Asad "remains unwilling to negotiate himself out of power" and "almost certainly intends to remain the ruler of Syria."[3] Iran and Hezbollah share that objective and continue to invest heavily in Syria on Asad's behalf. That testimony noted that infighting among anti-Asad groups has given government forces and their supporters an advantage in some areas, but that an overall stalemate is likely to prevail in the conflict for the foreseeable future.[4]

As clashes and diplomatic discussions continue, Syrian civilians continue to suffer in what U.S. Director of National Intelligence James Clapper has described as an "apocalyptic disaster." U.N. sources report that since March 2011, the conflict has driven more than 2.8 million Syrians into neighboring countries as refugees (out of a total population of more than 22 million; see **Figure 1**). According to U.S. officials, more than 6.5 million Syrians are internally displaced. The United States is the largest bilateral provider of humanitarian assistance, with more than $2 billion allocated to date.[5] In December 2013, the U.N. Office for the Coordination of Humanitarian Assistance (UNOCHA) appealed for an additional $6.5 billion in humanitarian assistance funding to respond to the crisis in 2014.[6] For more information on humanitarian issues, see CRS Report R43119, *Syria: Overview of the Humanitarian Response*, by Rhoda Margesson and Susan G. Chesser.

The negative effects of the humanitarian and regional security crises emanating from Syria now appear to be beyond the power of any single actor, including the United States, to independently

---

[2] Remarks by James R. Clapper, Director of National Intelligence, to the Senate Armed Services Committee, February 11, 2014.

[3] Office of the Director for National Intelligence, *Worldwide Threat Assessment of the U.S. Intelligence Community*, Senate Select Committee on Intelligence, January 29, 2014.

[4] Office of the Director for National Intelligence, *Worldwide Threat Assessment of the U.S. Intelligence Community*, Senate Select Committee on Intelligence, January 29, 2014.

[5] For details on U.S. humanitarian assistance see USAID, Syria Complex Emergency Fact Sheet #17, Fiscal Year (FY) 2014, June 19, 2014.

[6] For more information, see UNOCHA Syria Humanitarian Assistance Response Plan (SHARP) 2014 and 2014 Regional Response Plan (RRP).

contain or fully address. The region-wide flood of Syrian refugees, the growth of armed extremist groups in Syria, and the assertive involvement of Iran, Turkey, and Sunni Arab governments in Syria's civil war are negatively affecting overall regional stability. The war in Syria also is exacerbating local sectarian and political conflicts within Lebanon and Iraq, where violence is escalating and threatens national stability.

Policy makers in the United States and other countries appear to feel both compelled to respond to these crises and cautious in considering options for doing so that may have political and security risks such as the commitment of military forces to combat or the provision of large-scale material assistance to armed elements of the opposition. In light of these conditions and trends, Congress may face tough choices about U.S. policy toward Syria and the related expenditure of U.S. relief and security assistance funds for years to come.

Anti-Asad Forces

Syrian Opposition Coalition and Select Armed Elements

Anti-Asad forces have been engaged in a series of realignments and internal conflicts since mid-2013, creating complications for external parties seeking to provide support. To date, the United States has sought to build the capacity of the Syrian Opposition Coalition (SOC) and local activists. Many armed Sunni groups disavowed the SOC's participation in January-February 2014 talks with the Asad government in Switzerland. The U.S. government has recognized the SOC as the legitimate representative of the Syrian opposition and in May 2014 determined that the SOC's representative office in the United States would be considered a foreign mission pursuant to the Foreign Missions Act (22 U.S.C. 4301-4316).[7]

The other major component of U.S. assistance has been the provision of nonlethal and lethal support to armed groups in coordination with a Supreme Military Command Council (SMC), whose leadership has been in flux for much of 2014. In June 2014, several military officers reportedly resigned from the SMC, and Brigadier General Abdul-Ilah al Bashir al Noemi warned that U.S. support for individual armed groups risked creating "warlords."[8] General Salim Idris, the former leader of the SMC, and other commanders rejected leadership changes earlier in 2014 and have distanced themselves from the SMC's general staff and the SOC defense minister. On June 26, an interim government decision disbanding the SMC reportedly was issued and was rejected by Bashir and others.

Some reports suggest the Syrian Revolutionaries Front (SRF) and one of its prominent commanders, Jamal Maarouf, or individual elements formerly associated with the SMC may be emerging as focal points for new external assistance from the United States and others seeking to back relatively moderate armed opposition forces. In April 2014, a coalition of militia forces known as Harakat Hazm (Resoluteness Movement) released a video of their operatives loading

---

[7] According to an unnamed Administration official, the determination will not grant personnel of the office diplomatic immunity or convey control or ownership of Syrian state property under U.S. jurisdiction to the SOC. As of June 2014, the United States government had not formally withdrawn diplomatic recognition from the government of Bashar al Asad, although the State Department had expelled some Syrian diplomats from the United States.

[8] Dasha Afanasieva, "U.S. arms could create Syria 'warlords', rebel commander says," Reuters, June 9, 2014.

and firing what appeared to be U.S.-origin anti-tank weaponry in Syria.[9] Estimates of the coalition's size range from the hundreds to low thousands, and its leaders have made statements supporting secular and inclusive policy goals for a post-conflict Syria. Specific public information is lacking about which units or personnel within the coalition may have access to U.S.-origin weaponry, and several other armed groups have since posted social media material purporting to demonstrate their access to the same weaponry. An official affiliated with Harakat Hazm told the *New York Times* that "friendly states" had provided "modest numbers" of the weapons.[10] The commander of the group told the *Washington Post* that those who supplied the missiles had U.S. government approval and said the shipment "suggests a change in the U.S. attitude toward allowing Syria's friends to support the Syrian people."[11]

Asked about the reported shipments and use of U.S. origin weaponry by Syrian rebels, U.S. National Security Council spokeswoman Bernadette Meehan said, "The United States is committed to building the capacity of the moderate opposition, including through the provision of assistance to vetted members of the moderate armed opposition. As we have consistently said, we are not going to detail every single type of our assistance."[12] On May 5, an unnamed senior Administration official reiterated that formulation to members of the press in a background briefing, while stating that "asymmetry which exists on the ground militarily, unfortunately, between the regime and the moderate opposition is problematic for the emergence of the kinds of political conditions necessary for a serious political process. And we and others are focused on that."[13] On May 28, President Obama said, "I will work with Congress to ramp up support for those in the Syrian opposition who offer the best alternative to terrorists and brutal dictators."[14] In June, the Administration requested funding and authority to arm and train vetted opposition forces for select purposes after endorsing a Senate Armed Services Committee proposal contained in Section 1209 of S. 2410.

Section 3(a)(2) of the Arms Export Control Act (22 U.S.C. 2753 (a)(2)) applies obligations, restrictions, and possible penalties for misuse of U.S.-origin equipment to any retransfer by foreign recipients of U.S.-supplied defense articles, defense services, and related technical data to another nation. If such a retransfer occurred in the absence of prior U.S. approval, then the nation making such a transfer could be determined to be in violation of its agreement with the United States not to take such an action without prior consent from the U.S. government, with possible penalties as described in the act.

Armed Islamist Groups

In late 2013, a number of powerful Islamist militia groups—some of which formerly recognized the leadership of Idris and the SMC—announced the formation of a new Islamic Front.[15] The

---

[9] See Harakat Hazm YouTube Channel, April 15, 2014, at http://www.youtube.com/watch?v=5x5Q4aTGvu0.

[10] Ben Hubbard, "Syrian Election Announced; Rebels Report New Weapons," *New York Times*, April 21, 2014.

[11] Liz Sly, "Syrian rebels who received first U.S. missiles of war see shipment as 'an important first step,'" *Washington Post*, April 27, 2014.

[12] Tom Bowman and Alice Fordham, "CIA Is Quietly Ramping Up Aid To Syrian Rebels, Sources Say," National Public Radio (Online), April 23, 2014

[13] Transcript of Background Briefing on Syria by Senior Administration Official, U.S. State Department, May 5, 2014.

[14] Transcript of President Obama's Commencement Address, U.S. Military Academy, May 28, 2014.

[15] The following armed groups constitute the core of the Islamic Front and were the original signatories of its charter: Ahrar al Sham Islamic Movement; Suqur al Sham Brigades; Ansar al Sham Battalions; Jaysh al Islam; Liwa al Tawhid; (continued...)

Islamic Front and other recently created opposition coalitions active in northern Syria moved to evict ISIL from areas of northern and western Syria in January 2014 and remain engaged in hostilities with ISIL forces in some areas. Prior to the outbreak of the confrontation with ISIL, many expert observers considered the Front to be the most powerful element of the armed opposition in northern Syria. The pressures of confrontation between members of the Islamic Front and ISIL may be undermining the cohesion of the group, as differences in ideology, strategy, priorities, and preferred tactics encourage individuals, units, and groups within the Front to reconsider their positions.

The Front's November 2013 charter declared its goals to include "the full overthrow of the Al Asad regime in Syria and for building an Islamic state ruled by the sharia of God Almighty alone."[16] In that document, the Front explicitly rejected the concepts of secularism and a civil state, rejected "foreign dictates," and stated its commitment to maintaining the territorial integrity of Syria. Front leaders have rejected the SOC and issued a statement on January 20 in conjunction with the Mujahedin Army and another group rejecting the Geneva II talks and setting a series of conditions that must be achieved before they will contemplate a settlement.[17] The statement calls for "the entire regime, including its head and all its criminal figures" to step down and calls for security bodies to be held legally accountable. The Front and its allies further demand that there be "no interference in the form of the future state after the regime [steps down] and no imposition of any matter that conflicts with the Islamic identity of the masses or which takes away the rights of any section of society." A "Revolutionary Code of Honor" issued by the Front and other groups in May 2014 drew criticism from some hard-line Islamist figures for not explicitly calling for an Islamic state for post-Asad Syria. The Islamic Front sought to forbid its supporters from participating in the June 2014 presidential election, but also forbid attacks on polling stations and encouraged its supporters not to consider voters to be infidels.

Jabhat al Nusra, an Al Qaeda-affiliated militia and U.S.-designated Foreign Terrorist Organization, first sought to mediate between ISIL and its adversaries, but is now in outright conflict with ISIL (see **Figure 2** for a timeline of the emergence of the groups). Their confrontation is sending shockwaves through the global jihadist community as different clerics, armed group leaders, and individual supporters declare their respective views on the infighting. In general, other Syrian opposition forces have viewed Al Nusra as more accommodating and cooperative than ISIL, including some groups who oppose Al Nusra's ideology. Some members of the Islamic Front and other non-Islamist opposition groups coordinate their operations with Jabhat al Nusra in different areas. The pressures of combat against ISIL and the incompatibility of political goals among the groups produce pressure for and against such coordination.

Secretary Kerry has accused the Asad government of "funding some of those extremists—even purposely ceding some territory to them in order to make them more of a problem so he can make the argument that he is somehow the protector against them."[18] Several press reports allege that

---

(...continued)

and Liwa al Haqq.

[16] Charter of the Islamic Front. For translation, see U.S. Government Open Source Center (OSC) Document TRR2013112671951889, Syria: New 'Islamic Front' Formation Releases Charter, November 26, 2013.

[17] The signatories—The Islamic Front, the Mujahedin Army, and the Islamic Union for the Soldiers of the Levant— refer to themselves as the "forces active on the ground" in contrast to "those who only represent themselves." OSC Document TRR2014012066474330, "Syria: IF, Others Reject Regime Presence at Geneva 2, Issue Conditions for Political Solution," January 20, 2014.

[18] Ben Hubbard, "Syria Proposes Aleppo Cease-Fire…" *New York Times*, January 17, 2014.

opposition groups have sold oil and petroleum products from areas under their control to agents of the Syrian government. The Asad government's past permissiveness toward anti-U.S. Sunni extremist groups during the U.S. presence in Iraq and Asad's release of several prominent extremists from prison in 2011 raise further questions about the regime's strategy.

The intra-opposition battles have drawn increased global attention to the composition and direction of the Syrian opposition and the provision of external support to its armed elements. The formation of the Islamic Front in November 2013 raised questions about which forces actually remained affiliated with the SMC and whether they are credible partners for the United States and others. Then, in December, Islamic Front fighters took control of facilities and equipment belonging to the U.S.-backed SMC, including some U.S.-supplied materiel. The incident, the Front's continued rejection of the U.S.-preferred strategy of negotiation, and the group's long-term goal of establishing an Islamic state in Syria raise fundamental questions about whether and how the United States should engage with the Front and its allies.

In a January 2014 communiqué from their meeting in Paris, the United States and other members of the "Friends of Syria core group of countries" (aka the "London 11" or "Core Group")[19] stated that "all armed groups must respect democratic and pluralistic values, recognize the political authority of the National Coalition [SOC] and accept the prospect of a democratic transition negotiated in Geneva.... "[20] It remains to be seen whether statements by the Islamic Front and others rejecting secular democracy, the political authority of the SOC, and negotiations with the Asad government will preclude engagement by outsiders with the Front and its allies against Al Qaeda-affiliated groups in Syria or against pro-Asad forces.

Terrorist Threats Posed by Syria- and Iraq-Based Sunni Extremists

Since January 2014, U.S. officials have made several public statements describing the potential for Syria-based extremists to pose a direct terrorist threat to the United States. U.S. and European officials have highlighted the particular threat posed by foreign fighters, some of whom hold U.S. and European passports. Central Intelligence Agency Director John Brennan said in testimony before the House Permanent Select Committee on Intelligence in February 2014 that

> there are three groups of people that are a concern, from an extremist standpoint; Ahrar al Sham, Jabhat al Nusra, which is the Al Qaeda element within Syria, and the Islamic State of Iraq and the Levant (ISIL). It's those latter two I think are most dedicated to the terrorist agenda. We are concerned about the use of Syrian territory by the Al Qaeda organization to recruit individuals and develop the capability to be able not just to carry out attacks inside of Syria, but also to use Syria as a launching pad. So it's those elements—Al Qaeda and ISIL - that I'm concerned about, especially the ability of these groups to attract individuals from other countries, both from the West, as well as throughout the Middle East and South Asia, and with some experienced operatives there who have had experience in carrying out a global jihad.... There are camps inside of both Iraq and Syria that are used by Al Qaeda to develop capabilities that are applicable, both in the theater, as well as beyond.[21]

---

[19] The group consists of Egypt, France, Germany, Italy, Jordan, Qatar, Saudi Arabia, Turkey, the United Arab Emirates, the United Kingdom, and the United States.

[20] Foreign Ministry of France, Declaration of the Core Group Ministerial Meeting on Syria, Paris, January 12, 2014.

[21] Testimony of CIA Director John Brennan, House Permanent Select Committee on Intelligence, February 5, 2014.

Brennan called the threat posed by these groups "a near-term concern, as well as a long-term concern," and said that "the intelligence community, including CIA, is working very closely with our partners internationally to try to address the terrorist challenge." In press reports, unnamed intelligence officials have described the foreign fighter problem as "one of the most significant threats we're dealing with," and the Federal Bureau of Investigation reportedly is monitoring several returnees from Syria. Homeland Security Secretary Jeh Johnson has called the terrorist threat from Syria "a matter of homeland security."

Islamic State of Iraq and the Levant (ISIL, a.k.a. ISIS)

The Islamic State of Iraq and the Levant (ISIL, also referred to as ISIS) is a transnational Sunni Islamist insurgent and terrorist group that has expanded its control over areas of northwestern Iraq and northeastern Syria since 2013, threatening the security of both countries and drawing increased attention from the international community. The group's ideological and organizational roots lie in the forces built and led by the late Abu Musab al Zarqawi in Iraq from 2002 through 2006—*Tawhid wal Jihad* (Monotheism and Jihad) and Al Qaeda in the Land of the Two Rivers (aka Al Qaeda in Iraq, or AQ-I). Following Zarqawi's death at the hands of U.S. forces in June 2006, AQ-I leaders repackaged the group as a coalition known as the Islamic State of Iraq (ISI). ISI lost its two top leaders in 2010 and was weakened, but not eliminated, by the time of the U.S. withdrawal in 2011.

Under the leadership of Ibrahim Awad Ibrahim al Badri al Samarra'i (aka Abu Bakr al Baghdadi),[22] ISI rebuilt its capabilities. By early 2013, the group was conducting dozens of deadly attacks a month inside Iraq. The precise nature of ISI's relationship to Al Qaeda leaders from 2006 onward is unclear. In recent months, ISIL leaders have stated their view that "the ISIL is not and has never been an offshoot of Al Qaeda,"[23] and that, given that they view themselves as a state and a sovereign political entity, they have given leaders of the Al Qaeda organization deference rather than pledges of obedience.

In April 2013, Abu Bakr al Baghdadi announced his intent to merge his forces in Iraq and Syria with those of the Syria-based Nusra Front, under the name ISIL. Nusra Front and Al Qaeda leaders rejected the merger, underscoring growing tensions among Sunni extremists in the region. In July 2013, ISIL attacked prisons at Abu Ghraib and Taji in Iraq, reportedly freeing several hundred detained members and shaking international confidence in Iraq's security forces. ISIL continued a fierce wave of attacks across northern, western, and central Iraq, while in Syria the group consolidated control over the city and province of Raqqa and expanded its presence in northwestern areas then-controlled by other rebel forces.

Late 2013 saw the Iraqi government seeking expanded counterterrorism and military assistance from the United States, ostensibly to meet the growing ISIL threat. Inside Syria, ISIL alienated its rebel counterparts further, and an anti-ISIL campaign erupted there in early 2014, expelling the group from some areas it had controlled and unleashing a cycle of ongoing infighting. ISIL remains strongest in Raqqah and Syria's eastern provinces of Dayr az Zawr and Hasakah, adjacent to western Iraq.

---

[22] Al Baghdadi was arrested and detained by U.S. forces in Iraq at Camp Bucca, until his release in 2009.

[23] OSC Report TRN2014051234500562, "Al-Furqan Releases ISIL Al-Adnani's Message Criticizing Al-Zawahiri, Refusing To Leave Syria," Twitter, May 11-2, 2014.

Figure 2. Evolution of Select Extremist Forces in Iraq and Syria, 2002-2014

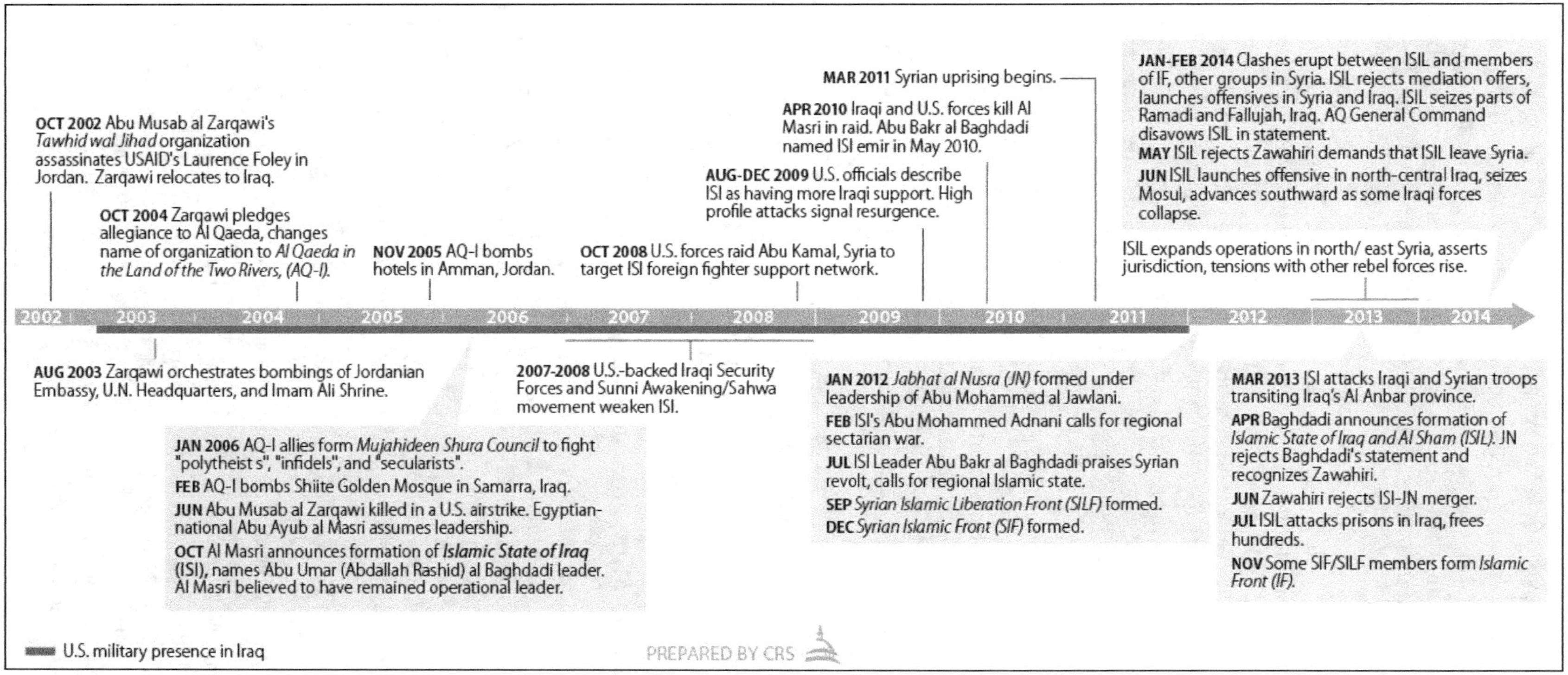

OCT 2002 Abu Musab al Zarqawi's *Tawhid wal Jihad* organization assassinates USAID's Laurence Foley in Jordan. Zarqawi relocates to Iraq.

OCT 2004 Zarqawi pledges allegiance to Al Qaeda, changes name of organization to *Al Qaeda in the Land of the Two Rivers, (AQ-I)*.

AUG 2003 Zarqawi orchestrates bombings of Jordanian Embassy, U.N. Headquarters, and Imam Ali Shrine.

JAN 2006 AQ-I allies form *Mujahideen Shura Council* to fight "polytheists", "infidels", and "secularists".

FEB AQ-I bombs Shiite Golden Mosque in Samarra, Iraq.

JUN Abu Musab al Zarqawi killed in a U.S. airstrike. Egyptian-national Abu Ayub al Masri assumes leadership.

OCT Al Masri announces formation of *Islamic State of Iraq (ISI)*, names Abu Umar (Abdallah Rashid) al Baghdadi leader. Al Masri believed to have remained operational leader.

2007-2008 U.S.-backed Iraqi Security Forces and Sunni Awakening/Sahwa movement weaken ISI.

NOV 2005 AQ-I bombs hotels in Amman, Jordan.

OCT 2008 U.S. forces raid Abu Kamal, Syria to target ISI foreign fighter support network.

MAR 2011 Syrian uprising begins.

APR 2010 Iraqi and U.S. forces kill Al Masri in raid. Abu Bakr al Baghdadi named ISI emir in May 2010.

AUG-DEC 2009 U.S. officials describe ISI as having more Iraqi support. High profile attacks signal resurgence.

JAN 2012 *Jabhat al Nusra (JN)* formed under leadership of Abu Mohammed al Jawlani.

FEB ISI's Abu Mohammed Adnani calls for regional sectarian war.

JUL ISI Leader Abu Bakr al Baghdadi praises Syrian revolt, calls for regional Islamic state.

SEP *Syrian Islamic Liberation Front (SILF)* formed.

DEC *Syrian Islamic Front (SIF)* formed.

MAR 2013 ISI attacks Iraqi and Syrian troops transiting Iraq's Al Anbar province.

APR Baghdadi announces formation of *Islamic State of Iraq and Al Sham (ISIL)*. JN rejects Baghdadi's statement and recognizes Zawahiri.

JUN Zawahiri rejects ISI-JN merger.

JUL ISIL attacks prisons in Iraq, frees hundreds.

NOV Some SIF/SILF members form *Islamic Front (IF)*.

JAN-FEB 2014 Clashes erupt between ISIL and members of IF, other groups in Syria. ISIL rejects mediation offers, launches offensives in Syria and Iraq. ISIL seizes parts of Ramadi and Fallujah, Iraq. AQ General Command disavows ISIL in statement.

MAY ISIL rejects Zawahiri demands that ISIL leave Syria.

JUN ISIL launches offensive in north-central Iraq, seizes Mosul, advances southward as some Iraqi forces collapse.

ISIL expands operations in north/east Syria, asserts jurisdiction, tensions with other rebel forces rise.

2002 | 2003 | 2004 | 2005 | 2006 | 2007 | 2008 | 2009 | 2010 | 2011 | 2012 | 2013 | 2014

U.S. military presence in Iraq

PREPARED BY CRS

Source: U.S. government reporting and U.S. Government Open Source Center (OSC) reports.

CRS-9

ISIL's attempts to assert control over the cities of Fallujah and Ramadi in Iraq's Al Anbar province and its June 2014 offensive in northern Iraq underscored the group's lethality and ability to conduct combat operations and manage partnerships with local groups in multiple areas over large geographic distances. The durability of ISIL's partnerships is questionable given its conflicts in Syria and past opposition from tribal, Islamist, and Baathist armed groups in Iraq.

Statements and media materials released by ISIL reflect an uncompromising, exclusionary worldview and a relentless ambition. Statements by Abu Bakr al Baghdadi and ISIL's spokesman Abu Mohammed al Adnani feature sectarian calls for violence and identify Shiites, non-Muslims, and unsupportive Sunnis as enemies in the group's struggle to establish "the Islamic State" and to revive their vision of "the caliphate."[24] The group describes Iraqi Shiites derogatorily as "rejectionists" and "polytheists" and paints the Iraqi government of Nuri al Maliki as a puppet of Iran. Similar ire is aimed at Syrian Alawites and the Asad government, although some sources allege that ISIL operatives have benefitted from evolving financial and security arrangements with Damascus dating back to the time of the U.S. presence in Iraq.

Deputy Assistant Secretary of State for Iraq Brett McGurk told the House Foreign Affairs Committee in February 2014 that ISIL's objective is "to cause the collapse of the Iraqi state and carve out a zone of governing control in the western regions of Iraq and eastern Syria." ISIL has since built upon what McGurk described then as its "unprecedented" resources in terms of funds, weapons, and personnel. Senior U.S. officials have stated that ISIL poses a serious threat to the United States and maintains training camps in Iraq and Syria, but presently lacks the capability to carry out operations on U.S. territory.[25] In July 2012, ISIL leader Abu Bakr al Baghdadi warned U.S. leaders that "the mujahidin have set out to chase the affiliates of your armies that have fled.... You will see them in your own country, God willing. The war with you has just begun."[26] In January 2014, Al Baghdadi threatened the United States directly, saying, "Know, O defender of the Cross, that a proxy war will not help you in the Levant, just as it will not help you in Iraq. Soon, you will be in direct conflict—God permitting—against your will."[27]

Potential Effects of ISIL Operations in Iraq on Syria[28]

ISIL gains in Iraq are likely to facilitate the flow of weapons and fighters into eastern Syria to ISIL and other groups, and may increase bilateral cooperation between the Maliki and Asad governments. Captured U.S.-origin military equipment provided to Iraqi security forces already has appeared in photos reportedly taken in Syria and posted on social media outlets. ISIL advances in Iraq could weaken the Syrian government's ability to hold ground in contested areas, as some Iraqi Shia militants who had previously fought alongside Asad forces return home to combat ISIL.[29] Syrian forces in mid-June conducted air strikes against ISIL-held areas of Raqqah

---

[24] OSC Report GMP20130409405003, "ISI Emir Declares ISI, Al-Nusrah Front: 'Islamic State of Iraq and the Levant,'" Translated from *Ansar al Mujahideen Network*, April 9, 2013.

[25] Statements by Secretary of Defense Chuck Hagel, Chairman of the Joint Chiefs of Staff General Martin Dempsey, and Secretary of State John Kerry, June 2014. See also Testimony of Central Intelligence Agency Director John Brennan before the House Permanent Select Committee on Intelligence, February 2014.

[26] OSC Report GMP20120721586002, "Islamic State of Iraq Amir Calls on Sunni Tribes To 'Repent,'" July 21, 2012.

[27] OSC Report TRR2014011980831299, "Al-Furqan Establishment Releases Audio Statement by ISIL Emir Condemning 'War' Against Group," Translated from *Al Minbar al I'lami Jihadist Forum*, January 19, 2014.

[28] Prepared by Carla Humud, Analyst in Middle Eastern and African Affairs.

[29] "Seeing their gains at risk, Shiites flock to join militias, *New York Times*, June 13, 2014.

and Hasakah in coordination with the Iraqi government, according to the London-based Syrian Observatory for Human Rights.[30] Increased cooperation between Damascus and Baghdad could alter the dynamics in both conflicts. It could undermine ongoing U.S. efforts to encourage Iraqi leaders to press Asad to step down in favor of a transitional government. Increased Iraqi-Syrian cooperation could also make Baghdad less likely to comply with U.S. requests to crack down on Iranian overflights of weapons and equipment to Damascus.

It is unclear what impact ISIL gains in Iraq would have outside of eastern Syria. At least half of Syria-based ISIL fighters are Syrian or Iraqi tribesmen, according to a Syrian ISIL defector.[31] Like other segments of the Syrian opposition, Syrian tribes have at times been reluctant to expand engagement with government forces beyond their own local areas. Since early 2014, ISIL has concentrated its forces in Syria's northeast, and has largely avoided regular confrontations in the country's main urban areas in Syria's western half. Any Iraqi or U.S. efforts to disrupt or sever ISIL supply lines linking eastern Syria and western Iraq could benefit Syrian military and Al Qaeda-affiliated Nusra Front forces also operating in the area.

Pro-Asad Forces[32]

The Syrian government has continued military and security operations against insurgents while pursuing political measures intended to boost Asad's domestic and international legitimacy. Government forces continued operations in Aleppo and Damascus in an effort to isolate rebels and sever their supply lines.[33] The government since the beginning of the year has also conducted more than 40 local truces with rebel groups in besieged areas of Damascus, Damascus Countryside, and Homs that have allowed it to gain greater control in some contested areas.[34]

Syria in early June held presidential elections—the first since 1955 in which there has been more than one candidate.[35] Elections were held in all provinces except Raqqah in northern Syria, which remains under the control of ISIL.[36] Syrian government officials reported that Asad won with 88.7% of the vote—falling short of the 97% victory he claimed in the 2007 presidential referendum—giving him a third seven-year term in office.[37] Opposition leaders were effectively disqualified from running by Syria's revised election law, which stipulates that candidates must have maintained continuous residence in Syria for 10 years prior to nomination and hold no other nationality or prior criminal convictions.[38] Syria's Supreme Constitutional court put voter turnout

---

[30] "Syria pounds ISIS bases in coordination with Iraq," *Daily Star*, June 15, 2014.

[31] "Sunni fighters gain as they battle 2 governments, and other rebels," *New York Times*, June 11, 2014. See also, Jamestown Foundation, "The Tribal Factor in Syria's Rebellion: A Survey of Armed Tribal Groups in Syria," *Terrorism Monitor* Vol. 11, Issue 13, June 27, 2013, and, Nicholas Heras, "The Battle for Syria's Al-Hasakah Province," U.S. Military Academy Combatting Terrorism Center, *CTC Sentinel*, October 24, 2013.

[32] Prepared by Carla Humud, Analyst in Middle Eastern and African Affairs.

[33] "Syria: military bombards Aleppo," *Associated Press*, June 16, 2014.

[34] OSC Report LIR2014061158407788, "Syria: regime exploiting humanitarian crisis to win truce deals, gain ground," June 11, 2014,

[35] "Aftershocks of the Egypt Spring on Syria," *Asia Times*, April 25, 2012.

[36] "Syria plans presidential elections in summer; minister says Assad will likely be one of several candidates," *Wall Street Journal*, March 16, 2014.

[37] "Assad re-elected in wartime election," *Al Jazeera*, June 5, 2014.

[38] "Syrian presidential election law excludes most opposition leaders," *Reuters*, March 14, 2014.

---

at 73.4%, although some Asad opponents stated that they voted primarily to avoid retribution.[39] Syrian oppositionists, as well as the United States and the European Union, condemned the vote as illegitimate.[40]

The United States and other members of the Core Group on Syria had previously rejected Asad's candidacy, noting that a decision to hold presidential elections was inconsistent with the Geneva Communique's call for the establishment of a transitional governing body.[41] Although the Syrian government participated in the Geneva II negotiations, its representatives insisted that counterterrorism issues be addressed before any discussion of a potential transition. Asad appears disinclined to make concessions that would significantly undermine his hold on power, particularly if he assesses that his military ultimately can prevail over insurgents or at least hold them at bay. Asad may judge that his move to declare and destroy his government's chemical weapons has eased international pressure on his government, and that peace talks will further expose opposition divisions—perhaps thereby demonstrating that his government lacks a credible negotiating partner.

The Geneva II Talks

The January-February 2014 Geneva II talks brought many of the internal and external fault lines in the conflict into sharp relief. Divergent perspectives among Syrian parties to the conflict were reflected among their respective international backers. The negotiations failed to make progress toward the establishment of a transitional governing body (TGB), but provided an opportunity for some members of the U.S.-recognized National Coalition of Syrian Revolution and Opposition Forces (or Syrian Opposition Coalition, SOC) to demonstrate their capability to represent the interests of Syrians and potentially improve their standing with some of the disparate opposition forces engaged in fighting inside Syria. Nevertheless, other opposition groups, including several powerful Islamist militias, rejected the negotiations and stated their intention to keep fighting until their demands are met.

According to U.N. officials, the Syrian government delegation refused to engage in discussions aimed at establishing a TGB and sought to focus on the question of combatting terrorism. Syrian military operations, including attacks on rebel held areas of Aleppo using barrel bombs and other indiscriminate means, continued during the talks and killed hundreds of civilians. Prior to the talks, President Asad stated that the government had already laid out its peace initiative in January 2013.[42] Under the first stage of this plan, the Syrian armed forces would halt military operations as soon as regional countries stopped funding and arming the opposition and when the opposition itself ceased attacks.[43]

The United States and other members of the Core Group have reiterated their support for negotiations on the terms of the Geneva communiqué, while criticizing the Asad government for "obstruction" and praising the SOC delegation for its participation in the talks.[44] Syrian government representatives criticized what they viewed as the opposition delegation's unwillingness to fully discuss terrorism and its inability to make firm commitments on the actions of armed groups.[45] The Asad government appears unwilling to open discussions regarding any transitional arrangements until its concerns with regard to terrorism and anti-state violence are addressed. Opposition representatives acknowledge the threats posed by extremist groups, but view the establishment of transitional arrangements as necessary for undermining the legitimacy of violent extremist groups.

The potential for future talks is uncertain, although participants and international supporters on both sides characterized the end of the January-February round of discussions as a recess and agreed to a four point agenda to guide talks if they resume. The four agenda items, as described by Joint Special Representative for Syria (JSRS) Lakhdar

---

[39] "After Assad's election triumph, fear grips stay-at-home Syrians," *Reuters*, June 5, 2014.

[40] "Assad re-elected in wartime election," *Al Jazeera*, June 5, 2014.

[41] Joint Statement by the London 11 Countries, April 3, 2014.

[42] President Asad, interview with Agence France Press, Syrian Arab News Agency, January 21, 2014.

[43] Asad, speech at the Damascus Opera House, Syrian Arab News Agency, January 6, 2013.

[44] Secretary of State John Kerry, Geneva Conference and Situation in Syria, Washington, DC, February 16, 2014.

[45] Syrian Arab News Agency (SANA), "Al-Jaafari: we will spare no efforts to make Geneva rounds of talks a success with open-mindedness and a positive spirit," Damascus, Syria, February 16, 2014.

Brahimi, are (1) violence and terrorism; (2) the TGB; (3) national institutions; and (4) national reconciliation and debate.[46] Obama Administration officials have reiterated their shared view that once a Transitional Governing Body [TGB] called for by the Geneva communiqué is established by mutual consent and has full control over state security services, "Asad and his close associates with blood on their hands will have no role in Syria." United Nations Security Council Resolution 2139 reiterated the Council's endorsement of the Geneva communiqué and demanded that parties support its implementation "leading to a transition that meets the legitimate aspirations of the Syrian people and enables them independently and democratically to determine their own future."

Shia Armed Groups and Iranian Support for the Syrian Government

The involvement of Shia militias and Iran in the Syrian conflict has evolved since 2011 from an advisory to an operational role, with forces in some cases now fighting alongside Syrian troops. Lebanese Hezbollah and Iran have traditionally depended on the presence of a friendly government in Damascus to facilitate the transit of weapons from Iran to Hezbollah and to preserve their ability to challenge Israel. Hezbollah and Iranian roles in Syria appear designed to bolster Asad's ability to suppress the opposition but also to secure their interests in Syria in the event that the Asad government does not survive.[47]

Hezbollah

In August 2012, the U.S. Treasury Department sanctioned Hezbollah for providing training, advice, and logistical support to the Syrian government.[48] U.S. officials also noted that Hezbollah has helped the Syrian government push rebel forces out of some areas in Syria. Hezbollah Secretary General Hassan Nasrallah, who was personally sanctioned for his role in overseeing Hezbollah's assistance to Damascus, publicly acknowledged Hezbollah's involvement in Syria in May 2013. Nasrallah also recently expressed confidence that the risk of the Asad regime's defeat and the partition of Syria had passed even if a war of attrition may persist.[49] He further referred to the need for reconciliation initiatives to bolster the Asad government's support among Syrians.

As of June 2014, Hezbollah fighters remained engaged in operations in the Qalamoun region northwest of Damascus, where the departure of some Iraqi paramilitary forces could place additional pressure on the group.[50] A senior Israeli military official in March 2014 stated that Hezbollah currently maintains 4,000 to 5,000 fighters in Syria.[51]

Over the past year, Hezbollah has worked with the Syrian military to protect regime supply lines by helping to clear rebel-held towns along the Damascus-Homs stretch of the M-5 highway.[52] Hezbollah personnel in 2013 played significant roles in battles around Al Qusayr and the

---

[46] Press Conference, Joint Special Representative for Syria Lakhdar Brahimi, Geneva, Switzerland, February 15, 2014.

[47] "Iran and Hezbollah build militia networks in Syria in event that Asad falls," *Washington Post*, February 10, 2013.

[48] E.O. 13582, U.S. Department of Treasury, August 10, 2012.

[49] "Hezbollah leader Nasrallah vows to keep fighters in Syria," *BBC*, February 16, 2014; and, OSC Report LIR2014040766062493, "Lebanon's Nasrallah to Al-Safir: Risk of Bombings Drops, Danger of Syrian Regime's Fall Ends," *Al Safir* Online (Beirut), April 7, 2014.

[50] "ISIS' Iraq offensive could trigger Hezbollah to fill gap left in Syria," *Daily Star*, June 16, 2014.

[51] "Israel watches warily as Hezbollah gains battle skills in Syria," *New York Times*, March 10, 2014.

[52] "Syrian Army goes all-in to take back strategic highway," *Christian Science Monitor*, December 2, 2013.

Qalamoun Mountains region, in which rebel presence along the highway threatened the government's ability to move forces and to access predominantly Alawite strongholds on the coast.[53] Hezbollah forces on the Lebanese side of the border reportedly monitor and target rebel positions near the border that facilitate attacks in Syria and Lebanon.

Last year saw an uptick in violence against Hezbollah targets in Lebanon, and the militia's support for the Asad government appears to be contributing to the rise in sectarian violence and tension in Lebanon. Jabhat al Nusra and ISIL have claimed responsibility for attacks on Hezbollah-controlled areas of Beirut and eastern Lebanon, describing the attacks as retaliation for Hezbollah's intervention in Syria.[54]

Iraqi Militias

Analysts estimate that there are between 2,000 and 5,000 Iraqi Shia fighting in Syria on behalf of the Syrian government.[55] Many hail from Iraqi Shia political and militia groups including Asa'ib Ahl al Haq and Kata'ib Hezbollah. Members identify their objective as the defense of Shia holy sites such as the tomb of Sayyida Zeinab, the granddaughter of the Prophet Mohammad, in southern Damascus. Other reports describe these groups as assuming a broad operational role, noting that militias have formed sniper teams, led ambushes, established checkpoints, and provided infantry support for Syrian armored units.[56]

It is difficult to assess the motivations of individual Iraqi fighters in Syria or determine whether Asad's survival is their primary goal. Some of the fighters appear to be young volunteers driven by a desire to protect Shia holy sites, while others are trained militiamen who previously fought coalition forces in Iraq. Reports suggest that Iraqi fighters receive training in Iran before being flown in small batches into Syria, and that they work closely with Lebanese Hezbollah.[57] However, it is unclear who ultimately exercises command and control over these militias. Clashes between Iraqi and local Syrian militias in mid-2013 resulted in some Iraqi combatants refusing to fight under Syrian command.[58] Recent gains by ISIL in Iraq have prompted some Iraqi fighters in Syria to return home and join local militias.[59]

Iranian Support

Since 2011, Iran has provided technical, training, and financial assistance both to the Syrian government and to pro-regime Shia militias operating in Syria. In February 2012, the U.S. Treasury Department sanctioned the Iranian Ministry of Intelligence and Security (MOIS) for providing substantial technical assistance to Syrian intelligence, noting that MOIS also participated in multiple joint projects with Hezbollah.[60] Treasury also designated the Islamic

---

[53] "Hezbollah and the fight for control in Qalamoun," Institute for the Study of War, November 26, 2013.

[54] "Hezbollah undeterred by ISIS claim, threats," *Daily Star*, January 6, 2014.

[55] "Leaked video: Iran guiding thousands of Shiite fighters to Syria," *Christian Science Monitor*, September 23, 2013; "From Qusair to Yabrud: Shiite foreign fighters in Syria," *Al Monitor*, March 6, 2014.

[56] "From Karbala to Sayyida Zaynab: Iraqi Fighters in Syria's Shi'a Militias," CTC Sentinel, August 27, 2013.

[57] "From Karbala to Sayyida Zaynab: Iraqi Fighters in Syria's Shi'a Militias," CTC Sentinel, August 27, 2013.

[58] "Iraqi Shi'ites flock to Assad's side as sectarian split widens," *Reuters*, June 19, 2013.

[59] "Seeing their gains at risk, shiites flock to join militias, *New York Times*, June 13, 2014.

[60] Department of the Treasury, Press Release, February 16, 2012.

Revolutionary Guard Corps-Quds Force (IRGC-QF) for training Syrian forces, and Iraqi Shia militias fighting in Syria have credited Iran for providing training and coordinating their travel into the country. Mohammad Ali Jafari, head of the IRGC, acknowledged in September 2012 that some members of the Quds Force were present in Syria,[61] and U.S. officials have described them as also working closely with Hezbollah. Regional observers in March 2014 estimated that between 1,000 and 1,500 IRGC members were present in Syria.[62] In terms of non-lethal aid, Iran has provided Syria with billions of dollars in credit to purchase oil, food, and import goods from Iran.[63]

Chemical Weapons and Disarmament: Background[64]

A major policy concern of the United States has been the use or loss of control of chemical weapons stocks in Syria during that country's ongoing civil war. The United States and other countries have assessed that the Syrian government has used chemical weapons repeatedly against opposition forces and civilians in the country. The largest-scale use to date was reportedly on August 21, 2013. The U.N. Mission to Investigate Allegations of the Use of Chemical Weapons in the Syrian Arab Republic released its report on September 16, 2013, concluding that surface-to-surface rockets containing the chemical weapons nerve agent sarin were used in the Ghouta area of Damascus against civilians on a "relatively large scale." The U.N. investigative mission was not tasked with assigning culpability for the attacks. Reports of attacks using chlorine gas in Hama province surfaced in mid-April 2014. The U.N. Fact-Finding Mission to investigate the allegations came under armed attack during an attempt to examine the site on May 27. The investigators concluded that the evidence they have been able to examine thus far "lends credence to the view that toxic chemicals, most likely pulmonary irritating agents such as chlorine, have been used in a systematic manner in a number of attacks."[65]

In August 2013, the Obama Administration threatened military action against Syria in response to chemical weapons use in Syria. In a diplomatic solution that resulted in the Administration withdrawing the threat, Syria agreed to join the international Chemical Weapons Convention (CWC), which requires Syria to destroy all of its chemical weapons stocks and production facilities and bans the use of any toxic chemicals in warfare. Based on a joint U.S.-Russian proposal, the Executive Council of the OPCW,[66] an intergovernmental body tasked with implementation of the CWC, approved a destruction plan under which Syria is required to destroy all chemical weapons by June 30, 2014. According to the Director General, Syria will not meet the June 30 deadline for destruction of all chemical weapons and production facilities,[67] but all declared chemical weapons agents have been removed from the country as of June 23, 2014. Syria is required to declare and destroy all of its chemical weapons stocks and production facilities under international supervision. Syria is believed to have possessed more than 1,000

---

[61] "Elite Iranian unit's commander says his forces are in Syria," *Washington Post*, September 16, 2012.

[62] "From Qusair to Yabrud: Shiite foreign fighters in Syria," *Al Monitor*, March 6, 2014.

[63] "Iranians dial up presence in Syria," *Wall Street Journal*, September 16, 2013.

[64] Prepared by Mary Beth Nikitin, Specialist in Nonproliferation.

[65] OPCW Office of the Director General, "Summary Report of the Work of the Fact Finding Mission in Syria Covering the Period from 3 to 31 May," June 16, 2014.

[66] The Organization for the Prohibition of Chemical Weapons, http://www.opcw.org.

[67] OPCW, "8% of Syrian Chemicals Still Remain to be Removed; Fact-Finding Mission in Syria; Some Progress on Syrian Production Facilities," June 17, 2014.

metric tons of chemical warfare agents and precursor chemicals. This stockpile included several hundred metric tons of the nerve agent sarin, which represented the bulk of Syria's chemical weapons stockpile. Damascus also had several hundred metric tons of mustard agent in ready-to-use form and several metric tons of the nerve agent VX.[68]

A joint mission of U.N. and OPCW personnel was created to monitor and facilitate Syrian chemical weapons disarmament.[69] OPCW-U.N. experts arrived in Damascus on October 1, 2013, and began to inspect Syria's declared chemical weapons facilities. The first stage of destruction activities focused on destroying "critical equipment" at chemical weapons production facilities. The OPCW spokesman told reporters on October 31 that the Syrian government met the November 1, 2013, destruction deadline for disabling production equipment, and that all chemical weapons stocks and agents in Syria were under "tamper-proof" seal.

Removal of Chemicals

The second stage of the chemical weapons destruction process involved transportation and removal of chemical weapons agents from the country. These are liquid chemicals that have not been loaded into delivery vehicles. The OPCW Executive Council on November 14, 2013, approved the destruction of Syria's chemical weapons agents ("priority 1" chemicals) outside of Syria due to the security situation in the country. The United States and others have provided equipment to the OPCW-U.N. Joint Mission to help safely transfer these chemicals from storage facilities to the Syrian port of Latakia. Once the chemicals arrived at the port, Danish and Norwegian ships picked up the chemicals and removed them from Syria. The first quantity of priority chemicals was moved to the port of Latakia in early January 2014, and the last shipment was on June 23, 2014. This is the first time all of a country's declared chemical weapons agents have been removed from its territory.

No country had agreed to conduct destruction operations on its territory due to public concerns about the dangers of the material, but also due to the short timeline for destruction which in some cases would not have allowed for the required environmental and health impact assessments. Therefore, the United States offered to neutralize the liquid chemical weapons agents on board the Maritime Administration's Motor Vessel (MV) *Cape Ray* using newly installed field deployable hydrolysis systems (FDHS). This ship is expected to receive 700 metric tons of both mustard agent and DF compound, a key component in sarin.[70] U.S. personnel, including 64 Army chemical specialists, will run the operation. Once removed from Latakia, the most dangerous compounds in approximately 60 containers will be transferred to the *Cape Ray* at the Italian port of Gioia Tauro for destruction at sea in international waters. NATO has canceled cooperation with the Russian Federation on guarding the *Cape Ray* during chemical weapons destruction activities because of Russia's actions in Ukraine.[71] Less sensitive chemicals will be shipped to commercial

---

[68] See CRS Report R42862, *Chemical Weapons: A Summary Report of Characteristics and Effects*, by Dana A. Shea; and Center for Disease Control, "Facts about Sarin," May 20, 2013. http://www.bt.cdc.gov/agent/sarin/basics/facts.asp.

[69] See http://opcw.unmissions.org/.

[70] "Army to Destroy Syrian Chemical Weapons Aboard Ship," *Army News Service*, January 3, 2014.

[71] "NATO to cancel activities with Russia, step up military cooperation with Ukraine," *Stars and Stripes*, March 6, 2014.

processing facilities, for example in the United Kingdom. Companies in Finland and the United States were awarded contracts for processing the liquid waste from the destruction process.[72]

Syria did not meet the original deadline of December 31, 2013, for removal of these agents from its territory. According to the OPCW Director General, the delays were caused by "security concerns, the procurement and delivery of large quantities of packaging and transportation materials and equipment, and adverse weather conditions."[73] Reports in early January quoted a Syrian government official as saying two CW storage sites have been under attack.[74] The Syrian government also missed a February 5, 2014, deadline, raising questions about the intentions of the Syrian government. In February, the U.N. Security Council called upon Syria to expedite removal of the chemicals. The United States in particular had been critical of the slow progress by the Syrian government. As U.S. Ambassador to the OPCW Robert Mikulak said,

> The international community has put into place everything that is necessary for transport and destruction of these chemicals. Sufficient equipment and material has been provided to Syria. The ships to carry the chemicals away from Syria are waiting. The U.S. ship to destroy CW agent and precursors is now in the region and waiting. Commercial facilities to destroy other chemicals have been selected and contracts awarded; they are waiting. And yet Syria continues to drag its feet.[75]

In March, OPCW-U.N. Joint Mission Special Coordinator Sigrid Kaag described "important progress" in efforts to expedite the transfer and destruction of chemicals and encouraged the Syrian government "to sustain the current pace."[76] As of April 29, the Joint Mission estimated that the Syrian government had moved 18 shipments of chemicals to the port of Latakia, representing around 92.5% of total stocks to be removed (up from 53.6% in mid-March).[77] Ambassador Mikulak on April 29, 2014, said that "almost 100 tons of Priority 1 and Priority 2 chemicals still remain in Syria." He also said that the storage site where the remaining stocks were located was occupied by Syrian government forces and therefore packing and preparation for transport should have started immediately.[78] Fighting in the region of the site, which is northeast of Damascus, had raised concerns about the overland transportation of the materials. The Syrian government said the material could not be moved due to security concerns in the surrounding area. However, on June 23, 2014, the OPCW announced that it had supervised the removal of the final shipment of chemicals to the port of Latakia and they were successfully transferred and removed from the port.[79]

---

[72] "OPCW awards contracts to two companies for destruction of Syrian chemical and effluents," OPCW-U.N. Joint Mission Press Release February 14, 2014, http://opcw.unmissions.org/AboutOPCWUNJointMission/tabid/54/ctl/Details/mid/651/ItemID/182/Default.aspx.

[73] "Director General says Removal of Priority Chemicals in Syria Marks Important New Phase in Work of Joint Mission," OPCW press release, January 8, 2014.

[74] Nick Cumming-Bruce and Rick Gladstone, "Syrian Government Reports 2 Attacks on Chemical Arms Sites," *New York Times*, January 8, 2014.

[75] Robert P. Mikulak, "Statement to the Thirty-Ninth Meeting of the Executive Council," The Hague, Netherlands, February 21, 2014. http://www.state.gov/t/avc/rls/2014/221891 htm.

[76] "Over half of Syria's chemical weapons removed or destroyed, says joint OPCW-UN mission," UN News Centre, March 20, 2014.

[77] Ibid.; Secretary of State John Kerry Testimony before the Senate Foreign Relations Committee, April 8, 2014.

[78] Robert P. Mikulak, "Statement to the Fortieth Meeting of the Executive Council," The Hague, Netherlands, April 29, 2014.

[79] "Announcement to the media on last consignment of chemical leaving Syria," OPCW Press Release, June 24, 2014. (continued...)

Destruction of Production Facilities

The Syrian government also did not meet the deadline of March 15, 2014, for destruction of its 12 chemical weapons production facilities, and has proposed that the facilities not be completely destroyed but instead made inaccessible.[80] The CWC requires that production facilities be "physically destroyed." U.S. Ambassador to the OPCW Robert Mikulak said in a February statement that the Executive Council should require Syria to physically destroy the facilities in line with the Convention.[81] The OPCW has been developing a destruction plan for these facilities with Syria. Ambassador Mikulak said in a statement on April 29, 2014, that 12 chemical weapons production facilities declared by Syria remain "structurally intact," and Syria was not cooperating with the Technical Secretariat to resolve the issue. Mikulak noted that Syria should be held to the same standards as other countries that have destroyed their chemical weapons facilities, such as the United States. As of June 17, 2014, Syria has agreed to comply with the methodology for destroying the above-ground chemical weapons productions facilities in hangars, according to the Director General. There has been no resolution on destruction of the underground structures.[82]

U.S. and International Funding for CW Elimination Efforts

The international community, including the United States, is contributing both technical and financial assistance to the OPCW-U.N. Joint Mission. In-kind technical assistance to date includes specialized packaging from the United States for transporting chemical weapons in Syria, security-related support from Russia for Syrian ground movement of the materials, and cargo ships and naval vessels from Denmark and Norway.[83] Italy has volunteered to provide a port for transferring the agent from the cargo ships to the *Cape Ray*; the United Kingdom and Germany have provided a chemical processing facility for the destruction of some of the chemical materials.

According to the State Department, the United States has given approximately $6 million in financial assistance to the OPCW and U.N. joint mission through the State Department-administered Nonproliferation and Disarmament Fund. The United States has also given significant in-kind assistance to international inspectors. The largest contribution to the international effort has come from the Department of Defense Cooperative Threat Reduction (CTR) Program. On April 8, Deputy Assistant Secretary of Defense for Countering Weapons of Mass Destruction Rebecca K.C. Hersman said that the CTR program had allocated $160 million to support the CW elimination effort. DOD CTR also accepted $19 million in contributions from Germany, the UK, and Canada to assist with CTR programs, including the effort in Syria. Since the bulk of this funding was spent preparing the MV *Cape Ray* and equipping inspectors, the

---

(...continued)

http://www.opcw.org/news/article/announcement-to-media-on-last-consignment-of-chemicals-leaving-syria/.

[80] "Syria to miss deadline to destroy 12 chemical arms sites," *Reuters*, March 6, 2014.

[81] Robert Mikulak, "Statement to the Thirty-Ninth Meeting of the Executive Council," The Hague Netherlands, February 21, 2014. http://www.state.gov/t/avc/rls/2014/221891 htm.

[82] OPCW, "8% of Syrian Chemicals Still Remain to be Removed; Fact-Finding Mission in Syria; Some Progress on Syrian Production Facilities," June 17, 2014. https://www.opcw.org/news/article/8-of-syrian-chemicals-still-remain-to-be-removed-fact-finding-mission-in-syria-some-progress-on-s/.

[83] "Frequently Asked Questions," OPCW website, http://www.opcw.org/special-sections/syria-and-the-opcw/frequently-asked-questions/.

budget request for FY2015 is less than what was spent this past year—$15.7 million for technical expertise and resources to support the U.N.-OPCW Joint Mission in FY2015.

For more information on Syria's chemical weapons and U.S. and international participation in the disarmament process, see CRS Report R42848, *Syria's Chemical Weapons: Issues for Congress*, coordinated by Mary Beth D. Nikitin.

U.S. Policy and Assistance

Debates over U.S. policy toward Syria since 2011 have repeatedly returned to the question of U.S. military intervention, whether to protect civilians, target terrorist groups, or punish Syrian forces suspected of involvement in chemical weapons attacks or other attacks on opposition-held areas. To date, Administration officials have stated that U.S. military intervention to shape the outcome of Syria's civil conflict or to change the Syrian regime may not achieve U.S. objectives, and may lead to unintended negative consequences. Administration officials have cited a number of reasons for their reluctance to undertake direct military intervention or provide large-scale assistance to shift the balance of power in Syria, including fears of exacerbating the violence; inviting greater regional spillover or intervention; or opening a power vacuum that could benefit the extremists who are part of the opposition.[84] Uncertain costs, military constraints, and domestic political opposition to such involvement also are likely factors.

Some critics of the Administration's policy argue that many of these negative outcomes are occurring even in the absence of U.S. intervention and suggest that the image and influence of the United States are weakened by a refusal to intervene to protect civilians or respond to provocations. Others express concern that military intervention will exacerbate negative conditions prevailing on the ground and suggest that the United States cannot ensure that intervention or support provided to opposition groups will not benefit extremists.

Recent Administration official statements concerning potential terrorist threats emanating from Syria have led to a reconsideration of many of these questions by some Members of Congress and the public. The Administration's June 2014 request for funding and authority to arm and train vetted Syrian opposition forces signaled that such a reconsideration indeed has taken place. However, Administration officials maintain that U.S. policy goals and the contours of the United States' declared policy goals and preferred means have not fundamentally changed.

While condemning Asad as a thug and a murderer and aiding some of his adversaries, Administration officials have continued to stress the need for a negotiated political solution to the conflict in the hopes of keeping the Syrian state intact, securing its weapon stockpiles and borders, and combating extremist groups now active there. The implementation of U.S. strategy in Syria to date has included the provision of both nonlethal and lethal assistance to select Syrian opposition groups, a sustained international diplomatic effort to establish a negotiated transition, and the provision of humanitarian assistance in Syria and neighboring countries. Through 2013, these initiatives were implemented under the auspices of an ad hoc series of assistance notifications to Congress providing for the waiver of certain restrictions on the use of U.S. funds

---

[84] Other competing foreign policy priorities also have influenced the Administration's position, such as a desire to maintain Russian and Chinese support for international sanctions on Iran's nuclear program and concern that sectarian and strategic competition in Syria could ignite a regional conflict and threaten U.S. allies and global security interests.

for assistance in Syria and the assertion of emergency contingency authorities to reprogram and allocate funds for use in response to the crisis. In 2014, a shift toward independently authorized and funded assistance programs appeared to be underway. Cumulatively, the notifications and requests submitted to date illustrate an evolution of U.S. involvement in the direction of seeking deeper partnership with select opposition actors on the ground in Syria, while seeking to bolster and unify opposition figures based outside of Syria.

As of June 2014, the United States had allocated more than $287 million in support of the non-armed opposition (including the SOC and local activists), more than half of which had been delivered as of late March.[85] The delivery of some assistance to select groups resumed after having been suspended as a result of the Islamic Front's seizure of SOC/SMC-controlled warehouse facilities and intra-opposition fighting in northern Syria.[86] The FY2014 Consolidated Appropriations bill (H.R. 3547, P.L. 113-76) provided new authority for the Administration to use FY2014 and previously appropriated monies in the Economic Support Fund (ESF) account to provide nonlethal assistance for certain purposes in Syria.

FY2014 Consolidated Appropriations Act and Nonlethal Assistance in Syria

Section 7041(i) of Division K of the FY2014 Consolidated Appropriations Act (H.R. 3547, P.L. 113-76) significantly expands the Administration's authority to provide nonlethal assistance in Syria for certain purposes using the Economic Support Fund (ESF) account. Such assistance had been restricted by a series of preexisting provisions of law (including some terrorism-related provisions) that required the President to assert emergency and contingency authorities to provide such assistance to the Syrian opposition and communities in Syria. The new authority makes FY2014 and prior year ESF funding available "notwithstanding any other provision of law for non-lethal assistance for programs to address the needs of civilians affected by conflict in Syria, and for programs that seek to—

(A) establish governance in Syria that is representative, inclusive, and accountable;

(B) develop and implement political processes that are democratic, transparent, and adhere to the rule of law;

(C) further the legitimacy of the Syrian opposition through cross-border programs;

(D) develop civil society and an independent media in Syria;

(E) promote economic development in Syria;

(F) document, investigate, and prosecute human rights violations in Syria, including through transitional justice programs and support for nongovernmental organizations; and

(G) counter extremist ideologies."

The act requires the Secretary of State to "take all appropriate steps to ensure that mechanisms are in place for the adequate monitoring, oversight, and control of such assistance inside Syria," and requires the Secretary of State to "promptly inform the appropriate congressional committees of each significant instance in which assistance provided pursuant to the authority of this subsection has been compromised, to include the type and amount of assistance affected, a description of the incident and parties involved, and an explanation of the Department of State's response."

The act further requires the Obama Administration to submit a comprehensive interagency strategy prior to using the authority that would include a "mission statement, achievable objectives and timelines, and a description of inter-agency and donor coordination and implementation of such strategy." The strategy, which may be classified, must also

---

[85] See U.S. State Department Fact Sheet, U.S. Assistance and Support for the Transition, January 17, 2014; and Assistant Secretary of State for Near East Affairs Anne Patterson Testimony before the Senate Foreign Relations Committee, March 26, 2014.

[86] The State Department has reported that lines of supply for nonlethal support to armed opposition elements are "periodically contested by the regime or extremist fighters." In the wake of the incident the Obama Administration "decided that it was a risk to be providing that assistance if it's going to the extremists." See Secretary of State Kerry, Remarks with Qatari Foreign Minister Khalid bin Muhammad al Atiyah, Paris, France, January 12, 2014; and, Secretary of State Kerry, Press Availability at the Geneva II International Conference on Syria, January 22, 2014.

include "a description of oversight and vetting procedures to prevent the misuse of funds." All funds obligated pursuant to the new authority are subject to established congressional notification procedures.

FY2015 Budget Request for Syria

The FY2015 basic foreign assistance request for Syria reflects the two main elements of the Obama Administration's policy response: (1) humanitarian assistance to meet the needs of internally displaced Syrians and refugees in neighboring countries, and (2) political, economic, and non-lethal military support for national and local opposition groups. Funds provided since 2011 in Syria and in neighboring countries for these combined purposes exceed $2 billion to date.

Table 1. U.S. Foreign Assistance for Syria, FY2013-FY2015 Request

(In thousands of current dollars; fiscal year denotes source of funds)

Account	FY2013 (Actual)	FY2014 (Estimate)	FY2015 (Request)
ESF	20,780 (OCO)	n.a.	125,000 (OCO)
INCLE	0	n.a.	10,000 (OCO)
NADR	0	n.a.	20,000
PKO	38,620 (OCO)	n.a.	0
FFP	18,338	n.a.	0
Totalª	77,738	n.a.	155,000

Source: State Department and Foreign Operations, Congressional Budget Justification, FY2015.

Notes: FY2014 estimates for Syria spending were not available as of April 2014. Funds appropriated in fiscal years prior to FY2013 have supported U.S. assistance programs since 2011. n.a. = not available.

a. The FY2013 total figure does not reflect all of the $287 million allocated for support to the Syrian opposition to date. The FY2015 Syria request includes, but the table does not show, $1.1 billion within Migration and Refugee Assistance (MRA-OCO) and International Disaster Assistance (IDA-OCO) accounts expected to be used for humanitarian assistance related to the Syria conflict.

Of the total $1.26 billion in FY2015 funding requested specifically for Syria in the basic foreign operations budget request, $1.1 billion in Overseas Contingency Operations funds would support humanitarian response needs from the Migration and Refugee Assistance (MRA-OCO) and International Disaster Assistance (IDA-OCO) accounts. A further $155 million from the Economic Support Fund-Overseas Contingency Operations (ESF-OCO), International Narcotics Control and Law Enforcement-Overseas Contingency Operations (INCLE-OCO), and Nonproliferation, Anti-terrorism, De-mining, and Related Programs (NADR) accounts would support the Syrian opposition and transition related initiatives. If a transition should occur, FY2015 funds would support a political transition toward democracy, as well as reconstruction and recovery efforts. Specific proposals for the use of those funds are not yet available. The House version of the FY2015 State Department and Foreign Operations Appropriations bill would extend "notwithstanding" assistance authority for FY2015 funds, contingent on an update of the strategy required under P.L. 113-76.

Proposed Expansion or Restriction of Lethal and Nonlethal Assistance

Congressional Proposals

In the 113th Congress, proposals to authorize the expanded provision of nonlethal and lethal assistance in Syria with various provisos have been introduced or considered in committees, and would place various conditions on assistance, establish reporting requirements, grant diverse authorities, and set different time limitations. Most recently, the Senate Armed Services Committee reported version of the FY2015 National Defense Authorization Act (Section 1209 of S. 2410) would authorize the Department of Defense, with the concurrence of the State Department, to train and equip vetted members of select Syrian opposition forces for limited purposes through the year 2018. S. 960, the Syria Transition Support Act of 2013, was approved by the Senate Foreign Relations Committee as amended by a 15-3 vote in May 2013. H.R. 1327, the Free Syria Act of 2013, was introduced in March 2013. House and Senate Foreign Operations Appropriations bills under consideration for FY2015 would extend FY2014 authorities to provide non-lethal assistance in Syria for select purposes (S. 2499).

Section 10010 of the House-passed Defense Department appropriations bill for FY2015 (H.R. 4870) would prohibit the use of defense funds "to transfer man-portable air defense systems (MANPADS) to any entity in Syria." Other proposals, such as H.R. 2503 and H.R. 2432, seek to prohibit any military assistance to combatants in Syria.

Executive Branch Proposal—Syria Regional Stabilization Initiative

On June 26, 2014, the Administration released its request for FY2015 Overseas Contingency Operations (OCO) funds for the Department of Defense as well as additional requested funds for State Department programs. Included in the request were requested funds that would be designated for a proposed $1.5 billion Syria Regional Stabilization Initiative (RSI).[87] According to the RSI request, the Administration is seeking funding and authorization from Congress to do the following:

- Notwithstanding other provisions of law, through December 2018, "to provide assistance, including the provision of defense articles and defense services, to appropriately vetted elements of the Syrian opposition and other appropriately vetted Syrian groups or individuals for the following purposes:

  (1) Defending the Syrian people from attacks by the Syrian regime, facilitating the provision of essential services, and stabilizing territory controlled by the opposition;

  (2) Defending the United States, its friends and allies, and the Syrian people from the threats posed by terrorists in Syria; and

---

[87] Estimate #2—FY 2015 Budget Amendments: Department of Defense (DOD) and Department of State and Other International Programs (State/OIP) to update the FY 2015 Overseas Contingency Operations funding levels; for both DOD and State/OIP to implement the Counterterrorism Partnerships Fund and the European Reassurance Initiative; and for State/OIP peacekeeping costs in the Central African Republic. Available at http://www.whitehouse.gov/omb/budget_amendments.

(3) Promoting the conditions for a negotiated settlement to end the conflict in Syria."

If approved by Congress as requested, the authority would be supported by $500 million in FY2015 funding, presumably with requests in future years to follow. The requested authority would allow the U.S. government to accept foreign contributions to authorized efforts to provide such assistance.

- The request also seeks funding and authority for expanded efforts to "build the capacity of the Syrian opposition and of neighboring countries including Jordan, Lebanon, Turkey, and Iraq to manage the growing spillover effects of the Syrian conflict." According to the request, the Administration intends to use any funds provided by Congress for the RSI to "leverage existing security cooperation and assistance programs, expand training and related infrastructure, and tailor support packages to meet identified regional needs for areas contending with refugees and other destabilizing effects from the Syrian conflict."

Potential Questions for Congress

Potential questions of interest for congressional consideration and oversight of the RSI request may include the following:

- What effects might the provision of overt military assistance to non-state armed groups and individual combatants in Syria's non-international armed conflict have on U.S. efforts to discourage other actors from providing military assistance to the Syrian government or providing similar assistance to actors in other conflicts? What precedents, if any, would Congress be setting if it authorized and funded such an overt program?

- To which groups, entities, and individuals does the Administration intend to provide expanded assistance, including defense articles and services? What are their political goals for the future of Syria? What types of weaponry or training may be provided to recipients? What may not be provided? Why?

- What mechanisms will be put in place to monitor the disposition of any provided U.S. defense articles? What specific vetting criteria will be used to assess the worthiness of intended recipients? What conditions or criteria might prevent a group or individual from being eligible for U.S. assistance?

- Where will such training and equipping efforts take place? With what implications for the host country or countries? How does the Administration expect the current Syrian government and its allies to respond to those assisting any such U.S. efforts?

- How might the provision of overt military assistance to the Syrian opposition affect the willingness of the Asad government to cooperate on issues of importance to the United States, including counterterrorism, regional security, and the conflict in Iraq? How might the provision of U.S. military assistance to select groups affect the balance of power and political relations among different Syrian opposition groups?

- What countries are likely to contribute financially to potential U.S. efforts described the proposed request?

- How might the Administration intend to report to Congress on the status, achievements, and outstanding goals of such a program? What additional administrative and program management costs, if any, might be associated with the proposal?

Issues Shaping Future U.S. Assistance

As with humanitarian assistance, U.S. efforts to support local security and service delivery efforts to date have been hindered by a lack of regular access to areas in need. According to Administration officials, border closures, ongoing fighting, and risks from extremist groups have presented unique challenges. The infighting among opposition forces and the empowerment of ISIL in eastern Syria and north and western Iraq creates further complications. With the Administration now requesting funding and authority to provide overt lethal assistance to vetted elements of the Syrian opposition, the debate over the future nature and direction of U.S. engagement in Syria appears set to intensify.

To date, advocates of continued U.S. support for select opposition groups have argued that the withdrawal or reduction of such assistance would bolster less cooperative or friendly groups. Advocates have further argued that if the United States withdraws or reduces its support, then it may "force" moderate groups to turn to extremist groups for funding and support—thereby increasing the influence of extremists while reducing U.S. leverage. On the other hand, critics of continued or expanded U.S. support have argued that such assistance risks exacerbating rivalry among opposition groups and reducing the credibility of groups and individuals seen to be aligned with the United States. Critics of support also have pointed to problems in ensuring the identity of end users of provided support and the uses of U.S.-provided support.

The provision of overt military assistance would represent a significant evolution in U.S. efforts to support armed opposition elements. In June 2013, Deputy National Security Adviser for Strategic Communications Ben Rhodes said that the President had "authorized the expansion of our assistance to the Supreme Military Council," and Secretary of Defense Chuck Hagel said in a September 2013 hearing before the Senate Foreign Relations Committee that the Administration was taking steps to provide arms to some Syrian rebels under covert action authorities.[88] Press reports have cited unidentified U.S. officials suggesting that as of early October 2013, very little lethal equipment had been delivered and fewer than 1,000 opposition fighters had received U.S. supervised training in Jordan. CRS cannot confirm these reports. Press reports further suggested that the program was being enlarged to produce "a few hundred trained fighters each month,"[89] but it is unclear what effect, if any, recent developments, including infighting among opposition groups, have had on any such plans or programs.

---

[88] Secretary Hagel said, "it was June of this year that the president made the decision to support lethal assistance to the opposition. As you all know, we have been very supportive with hundreds of millions of dollars of non-lethal assistance. The vetting process that Secretary Kerry noted has been significant, but—I'll ask General Dempsey if he wants to add anything—but we, the Department of Defense, have not been directly involved in this. This is, as you know, a covert action. And, as Secretary Kerry noted, probably to [go] into much more detail would—would require a closed or classified hearing."

[89] Greg Miller, "CIA ramping up covert training program for moderate Syrian rebels," *Washington Post*, October 2, 2013; and, Adam Entous and Nour Malas, "U.S. Still Hasn't Armed Syrian Rebels," *Wall Street Journal*, September 4, 2013.

To date, U.S. officials have not publicly described in detail which elements of the opposition may be receiving training, what such training may entail, what types of weaponry may be provided in the program, and what safeguards may be in place to monitor the disposition of equipment and the actions of any U.S.-trained personnel. In late September, the Administration notified Congress of its intent to use emergency authorities available to the President under the Foreign Assistance Act to provide additional "nonlethal commodities and services" to the SMC. In January, the State Department referred to completed deliveries of food, medical equipment, and vehicles and "planned deliveries of satellite access equipment, laptops, radio communication equipment, and medical kits to moderate SMC elements" in a summary of its nonlethal support efforts to date.[90]

On October 22, 2013, Secretary Kerry said that the "London 11" group had "agreed to direct military aid exclusively through the Supreme Military Council ... to curtail the influence of extremists, to isolate the extremists, and to change the balance on the ground."[91] However, as noted above, several prominent Islamist militia groups now coordinate their operations independent of the SMC and have rejected the political and military leadership of the SOC/SMC. Disputes among former SMC commanders over its leadership also may complicate international efforts to engage with the SMC leadership as a conduit for support to moderate armed elements.

It remains to be seen whether these realignments, disputes, and policy statements have decisively changed the context in which the United States and its allies are providing support to the armed opposition, or whether or how such support may change in the near future. On April 8, 2014, Secretary Kerry told the Senate Foreign Relations Committee that "the fact is we are doing more than we've ever been doing." As noted above, the appearance of new weaponry in the hands of forces affiliated with SMC figures has raised speculation about changes in U.S. policy that may feature prominently in debate over the Administration's request to expand assistance further.

Outlook

Looking ahead, U.S. policy makers face a series of difficult choices as they seek to balance their demands that Asad ultimately leave power on the one hand, and their desire for the Syrian government to remain cooperative with implementation of the OPCW Executive Council decision, participate in negotiations with the opposition, and facilitate humanitarian access on the other. By seeking a negotiated rather than a military solution, U.S. policy apparently seeks to bring the conflict to a close while maintaining the security benefits associated with the preservation of some Syrian state institutions. However, recent statements by U.S. officials and other members of the Core Group envision negotiations that will end with the leaders of the current regime having no part in transitional governance in Syria.

In April, Secretary of State Kerry acknowledged that President Asad felt more confident in his position and alluded to a need to change the calculus of the Asad government and the opposition in order to bolster chances for successful negotiations. In testimony before the Senate Foreign Relations Committee on April 8, Secretary Kerry said:

---

[90] Office of the State Department Spokesperson, "The Syrian Crisis: U.S. Assistance and Support for the Transition," January 17, 2014.

[91] Remarks of Secretary of State John Kerry, London, United Kingdom, October 22, 2013.

Today, Assad feels fairly secure in Damascus and in some of the corridor going north to the ports. And that's been his strategy. But around him in the south, particularly, in the east and in the north, there is not that kind of security. In fact, the opposition has made some gains recently. And so the key here is - how do you get the parties to a place where they both understand that there isn't going to be a military solution that doesn't destroy the country absolutely and totally, but which ultimately could be negotiated? There has to be a recognition by both of the ripeness of that moment. It's not now. We all understand that. So the question is: Can you do something in order to create that? And that's a legitimate question for the Congress; a legitimate question for the Administration.

In May 2014, an unnamed senior Administration official reiterated the challenges posed to U.S. preferences by the prevailing military asymmetry in Syria and said, "while we continue to push for a genuine political solution, we also are focusing on doing what we can, together with the opposition, to try to address that asymmetry in various ways, to strengthen the opposition, and also to try to bring increased pressure of various types on the Asad regime."[92] The Administration's request for FY2015 OCO funding and authority to provide new military assistance to elements of Syria's opposition reflects these goals and perspectives.

Absent a change in conditions that compels Asad's departure or empowers opposition groups to fully depose Asad, current U.S. demands for a negotiated settlement leading to the establishment of a transitional governing body would appear to require the leaders of the current government to agree to leave power voluntarily, which they may continue to resist doing without guarantees of their safety and/or immunity. Opposition members may be unable or unwilling to make such guarantees. U.S. officials have raised the prospect of international peacekeeping arrangements to guarantee elements of a negotiated settlement, but such arrangements could require an international mandate, military forces, and financial contributions that may prove difficult to procure. Meanwhile, powerful armed Islamist opposition forces reject negotiation, seek the creation of an Islamic state, and have vowed to continue fighting until the entire Syrian government is toppled.

Reconciling the current U.S. diplomatic strategy and desire for cooperation on chemical weapons facility destruction with the simultaneous provision of U.S. assistance to select elements of the opposition may become more difficult in the event that negotiations begin and show promise, or in the event that anti-U.S. Islamist forces or Al Qaeda affiliates make further gains at the expense of their counterparts. The Obama Administration has yet to signal that ISIL's advances in neighboring Iraq have changed its calculus vis-à-vis the conflict in Syria.

In light of these conditions, responding to the humanitarian needs generated by the crisis and working to prevent the further destabilization of Syria's neighbors will remain key agenda items for U.S. decision makers for the foreseeable future.

---

[92] Transcript of Background Briefing on Syria by Senior Administration Official, U.S. State Department, May 5, 2014.

Author Contact Information

Christopher M. Blanchard, Coordinator
Specialist in Middle Eastern Affairs
cblanchard@crs.loc.gov, 7-0428

Carla E. Humud
Analyst in Middle Eastern and African Affairs
chumud@crs.loc.gov, 7-7314

Mary Beth D. Nikitin
Specialist in Nonproliferation
mnikitin@crs.loc.gov, 7-7745